"UNLOCKING THE GATES OF THE WATCH"

Whoever possesses the gates,
controls **everything!**

Malinda V. Robinson M.Ed.

ISBN- **978-0692204184**

Dedication

I *dedicate this book to God the Father, who is*

in heaven, Hollowed be your name. Your Kingdom come, your will be done, on earth as it is in heaven. (Mt 6:9-10)

To my incredible husband, my soul mate. Whom God divinely orchestrated our union. I love him dearly!

This book is also dedicated to our beloved daughter, Kayla Michelle Robinson, whose brief earthly life profoundly influenced our lives. You became the spiritual seed planted in the ground, giving life to our entire family. Daddy and I look forward to spending eternity with you.

To my beautiful children, KJ and Kenya who keep me sharp. It is because of them that I do what I do. I know that the decisions I make today will impact them. I am building a spiritual inheritance for them so that they will walk into all God has for them!

Table of Contents

Foreword

Unlocking the gates of the watch is a very insightful, inspiring, and practical approach to developing a richer and more fruitful prayer life. And I'm personally convinced that no matter what your level of maturity is at present in your walk with Christ, you will find this particular book to be one that will challenge you to achieve an even greater level of intimacy with God. What season of the watch are you in right now? Are you making the most of your time with God in prayer? These are questions that far too often go not only unanswered… But more often than not they go unasked. I believe it's time we all take a new stand as God's people to examine our prayer life in the light of James 5:16 to see if we are being both "effectual" and "fervent." My prayer is that this book will be a blessing to your prayer life as it was to mine…

Sincerely,

John Young
Senior Pastor of Empowered Believers Christian Learning Center

Foreword

In this book you will find strategic kingdom keys on how to advance the kingdom of God in your assigned region. God is releasing strategies to apostolic and prophetic voices in this hour on how to see whole cities and nations delivered. Malinda Robinson is definitely a prophetic voice for the hour that we live in. Amos 3:7 says "Surely the Lord GOD will do nothing, but he revealeth his secret unto his servants the prophets". I believe this book is a must have for all intercessors and prophets who are ready to advance the kingdom of God in their region and fulfill their divine assignment in the kingdom of God. God is moving swiftly with His church in this hour and those who have an ear to hear will hear and walk according to God's divine directives for the current season. The shift has taken place and a new standard for prophetic intercession is emerging at this time. This book is revolutionary in the area of prophetic intercession and it adds an apostolic dimension to prophetic intercession as it will cause the intercessor advance swiftly in the spirit to see permanent change. It's not enough to just pray, you need a strategy in order to advance and gain the ground that you're believing to occupy. This revelation given to Malinda will change the way you view spiritual warfare, the kingdom of God, and intercession as a whole. It's time to take the land and rule according to our original kingdom design.

Sincerely,

Apostle Lionel Blair
Senior Founding Leader of
Spirit of Elijah Ministries
soeministries.com

Introduction:

Unlocking the Gates of the Watch is a tool that will aid in helping believers understand what time they are at spiritually, and what strategies the Lord would have them to walk in. In order for us to be the overcomers He's looking for in this hour, we must take courage. Jesus states in John 16:33, *"These things I have spoken to you, so that in Me you may have peace. In the world you have tribulation, but take courage; I have overcome the world."*

Beloved, this book will empower you to unlock hidden mysteries concerning the many ways our enemy attempts to block and distort our destiny. In the spiritual realm, battles are occurring day and night. As long as there are evils to overcome and injustices to fight, spiritual warfare will continue to be our reality.

There is far more available to us than just maintaining our salvation. God is calling us to understand the deep things of His Kingdom like never before. The Lord desires to reveal himself in our lives in ways that will blow our minds! He reveals himself in direct proportion to the amount of hunger and thirst that we have for Him and His Kingdom. Just like in our natural bodies we eat when we are hungry, we drink when we are thirsty, for nourishment.   Well, in the spirit it's the same way.

Nothing happens in the Kingdom without a declaration. When things are spoken realities are created. Jesus says to us, "I will give you the keys of the kingdom of heaven; and whatever you bind on earth shall have been bound in heaven, and whatever you loose on earth shall have been loosed in heaven." Mt 16:19

Jesus has given us the ability to bind to the earth, what's already in the Kingdom because you can't bind something in time and then have it bound in eternity. The Lord will release revelation and understandings regarding His Kingdom.

I have learned that there are levels and measures of truth. There are things that are true, but there are things that are more true for lack of better words. For example: In the Old Testament, if you touched a leper, you became unclean. Why, because the primary revelation of the Old Testament was the power of sin. However, in the New Testament, if you touch a leper, the leper becomes clean. Why, because the New Testament's primary revelation is the power of

God's love. When Jesus would come to someone who was sick in body, he would release the dominion of his kingship over their physical being and disease would leave.

When the truth comes it does not cancel out previous revelation, it builds upon it… *it is precept upon precept, precept upon precept, line upon line, line upon line, here a little, there a little. Isa 28:10*

As the Lord increases our understanding of the Kingdom (Kingdom is the King's domain, the realm of his dominion), we too will be able to release the dominion of the Lord's kingship.

May this book be a resource to inspire you to a higher understanding of our call as gatekeepers. May you become spiritually hungry for more of Jesus. May the Holy Spirit enlighten you in your inner man and take care of any doubts you may have of His presence in your life. May the Holy Spirit bring life to the Word in your life and fill your words with power to boost your faith, your boldness, and your confidence.

Speak IT! God's Original Intent

God's plan for us is revealed in Genesis and fulfilled through the death/resurrection of Jesus. However, if we look at the beginning of Genesis chapter one, we see that God has a plan for all creation. In Genesis 1:3, we read that God begins to **SPEAK** to things. He speaks to darkness and says, "Let there be Light!" (Isn't it interesting how He spoke this before He created the sun?) He speaks, and says, *"Let there be an expanse in the midst of the waters, and let it separate the waters from the waters." And God called the space "sky." And God said, "Let the waters beneath the sky be gathered into one place so dry ground may appear."* And so it was. He speaks and trees, plants, animals and wildlife appear. We notice in these opening verses that God speaks into existence what He desires to see. Did you notice that in each instance where God spoke, the word went out and accomplished that which it was sent out to do and did not come back to him void?

One of the principles of the Kingdom of God is "*speaking to things*". You may say, "Well, that's God we are talking about, and where am I in all this?" When God said, "Let us make man in our image and likeness", God created mankind to look, behave, and operate like Him. We have been made to be like God!

We notice that God created things in the earth with the ability to reproduce after its own kind. In Genesis 2:7, *"And the Lord God formed man out of the dust of the ground, and breathed into his nostrils the breath of life, and man became a living soul."* I like how this verse reads in the following translation. Targum Onkelos an ancient Aramaic translation says this, "*and man became a speaking spirit like God"*. It uses the words "Ruach memallela" a breath of speech," that which differentiates man from the beasts — the power to talk. Through our words, we can sustain or destroy, heal or wound, express kindness or cruelty. *Proverbs 18:21: "Death and life are in the power of the tongue: and they that love it shall eat the fruit thereof. "* God starts and does everything through words. Like God, man is created as a speaking spirit and given dominion to rule.

God's position on rulership has never changed. Man's position changed when Adam fell. But the second Adam, Jesus, redeemed man from the curse (Galatians 3:13) and reinstated man back into rulership. We see this in Matthew 28:18 where Jesus said, *"All power is given unto Me in Heaven and in earth."*

Jesus held all power in His hands and then reinstated this power for rulership back to His body. Ephesians 1:22-23, *"And He put all things in subjection under His feet, and gave Him as head over all things to the Church, which is His body, the fullness of Him who fills all in all."*

Now that we have a better understanding of how we were created, let's take a brief look at angels. My goal in this is to build upon the importance of our assignment here on earth.

Let me start by saying this first about our enemy. The Lord disempowered Satan and then left him alive. It was part of his punishment. See Daniel 7:12. The enemy got cast down to a planet where the very thing he wanted is in about 7 billion people. He wanted to be like God, and sit in the assembly of the Almighty. We are, seated in heavenly places, and we are made in the image and likeness of God according to Gen. 3:15b

When God created angels, He did not create them in His image or likeness. They are spiritual beings without bodies that are messengers of God and are ministering to the heirs of salvation. They have specific purposes assigned to them. They are not of the same classification as we are for ours is a much higher class. I find it interesting that in Psalms 8:5 it says this: *For thou hast made him a little lower than the angels, and hast crowned him with glory and honor.* However, the word "angel" in this verse translates "*elohiym*" which is God so; it should read, "a little lower than God." I like the way it's stated here: *Hebrews 1:4 "Being made so much better than the angels, as he hath by inheritance obtained a more excellent name than they."* In Christ, our classification in God is to be just below God in the earth! We are created a speaking-spirit with the authority to act for God as his spokesman in the earth.

The Lord is looking for men and women who live in agreement with His Word and stand before Him as His spokesmen. We must understand the authority we have been given as believers when exercising our authority *over the fish of the sea, and over the fowl of the air, and over the cattle, and over all the earth, and over every creeping thing that creepeth upon the earth* and even the very "*powers of darkness*".

Jesus demonstrated how the authority of the kingdom of heaven has dominion over any condition on the earth.

Satan recognizes the power of spoken words and is constantly trying to get man to speak words that contaminate, defile and destroy. We're not subject to the enemy, he's subject to us. It's this truth that we need to know, because it will set us free (John 8:32). This truth will put us in a proper position that will change our condition. When your position is unchangeable, your condition has to change. When you know the truth that you have absolute authority and you walk in it the enemy will know it also.

Jesus demonstrated and taught by saying He only says what God says (John 8:12).

If Christianity means that we ought to follow in the footsteps of Jesus, then we ought to be saying only what God says.

Jesus said in Matthew 12:35-37, that:
"A good man out of the good treasure of the heart brings forth good things, and an evil man out of the evil treasure brings forth evil things. But I say unto you, that every idle word that men shall speak, they shall give account thereof, in the Day of Judgment. For by your words thou shall be condemned".

Our words can either secure our destiny or destroy it!

Kingly Authority

The word "*Kingly*" according to Merriam Webster's Dictionary is an adjective defined as: having royal rank.

The Word of God pronounces every born-again believer a king. *Rev. 1:5,6 And from Jesus Christ, who is the faithful witness, and the first begotten of the dead, and the prince of the kings of the earth. Unto him that loved us, and washed us from our sins in his own blood, And hath made us KINGS and priests unto God and his Father; to him be glory and dominion for ever and ever. Amen.*

Every believer has a responsibility to operate and to fulfill the function that God has placed us in as Kings and Priest in the earth.

Kingship is acting on your spiritual authority to invade, occupy and influence the world around you. It is fulfilling the first great commission. In John 14:12 the Lord said, *"Truly, truly, I say to you, he who believes in Me, the works that I do shall he do also; and greater works than these shall he do; because I go to the Father."* Jesus demonstrated this with His life, and this is what He has called us to walk in.

Kingship is our authority in Christ to exert His Lordship on the earth. By abiding in the King, we too can walk in authority over any condition on the earth. We are able to delegate His victory and dominion achieved in His death and resurrection.

Our first calling is to be like Him, and our second calling is to do the works that He did. Romans 13:1 states: *"Every person is to be in subjection to the governing authorities. For there is no authority except from God, and those which exist are established by God."*

As Christians, we must allow the Spirit of the Lord to move us under the authority of His domain in order for us to fulfill all that we were created for. Every person was designed to be under some form of authority. Jesus modeled this in His own life. He lived under the authority of His Father. He made no independent decisions.

The word "authority" in this scripture, is from the Greek word Exousia which means power of choice, liberty of doing as one pleases; the ability or strength with which one is endued, which he either possesses or exercises.

Godly authority begins with God. There is no authority except from God. Authority is bestowed upon us through relationship, and therefore it is only as deep as that relationship.

Authority also means, the power of rule or government (the power of him whose will and commands must be submitted to by others and obeyed); and used with reference to delegated authority in the form of a warrant, license, or authorization to perform.

Jesus was asked, *"By what authority are You doing these things, and who gave You this authority?"* (Matt 21:23). He was granted authority for his ministry from God the Father. *"No one has taken it away from Me, but I lay it down on My own initiative. I have authority to lay it down, and I have authority to take it up again. This commandment I received from My Father."* (John 10:18)

Jesus demonstrated His authority over disease, over nature, over demons, over sin and over death. These were the credentials of the King.

Jesus restored to us what Adam lost in the garden by defeating the devil; He whipped him, and made a public spectacle of him (Col. 2:15). He stripped Satan of all power and in turn gave it to the believer to be used under the authority of His name (Mark 16:17-20).

Jesus said, *"ALL authority has been given to Me in heaven and on earth"* (Matt. 28:18). As a priesthood of kings, we have been given the responsibility to steward the earth and establish the Gospel of the Kingdom, and the rule of God.

Like King David, we can run into battle exercising our kingly authority. When he heard the challenge of Goliath and saw the fear on the faces of God's warriors he boldly asked, *"Who is this uncircumcised Philistine that would challenge the armies of the living God?" (1 Samuel 17:26).*

So how are we to reign in this authority?

We reign through prayer; *With all prayer and petition pray at all times in the Spirit, and with this in view, be on the alert with all perseverance and petition for all the saints, Ephesians 6:18*

We are to reign by having an intimate relationship with God. Relationship is the heart of Kingdom authority. The Bible says, *" But seek ye first the kingdom of God, and his righteousness; and all these things shall be added unto you."* If we want to walk in spiritual authority, we need to put relationship with our Father first.

We are to reign by understanding that our authority is not based on our personal ability, strength or perceived worth: it is based on our understanding that we have been sent and authorized to be His representatives. We must be obedient to Him, to go and use His power in the manner that He has authorized.

We are to reign by understanding that our kingship ministry does not operate apart from priestly intercession. This is why we are called to be kings AND priests unto God and not kings OR priests.

Have you ever noticed that Jesus didn't entreat the Father to heal anyone? No, His prayers were short decrees of things that He already knew to be the Father's will. Jesus spoke that which He already knew was done in heaven, and brought heaven to earth by Kingly decrees. To a crippled man Jesus would say, "Arise and walk" or "Be healed." To a blind man Jesus would just say, "See," or to a deaf mute He would say "Be opened!" Even to a dead man Jesus just said, "Come forth!"

Had you ever realized before that in Christ YOU is the way through whom the Father desires to bring the Kingdom to the earth? Yes, we are it! There is no other plan!

Priestly Authority

How do we fulfill our roles as Priest? This question far too often goes not only unanswered... But more often than not the question goes unasked. I would like to spend some time on this question because I believe the Lord would have me to do so.

What is a priest? Merriam Webster's Dictionary defines a priest as one authorized to perform the sacred rites of a religion, especially as a mediatory agent between humans and God.

Now, let's look at the reason for the Levitical priesthood. As we know, Israel's Levitical priests performed ritualistic rites on behalf of the people. The Levitical priesthood was based on heredity. They officiated at the altar of the Tabernacle, giving burnt offerings and ritual sacrifice in the Holy place. The priests killed animals, ceremonially offering them on the temple altar to God to atone for the sins of the people. These imperfect sacrifices were given in order to bring sinful people back into communion with a Holy God. Priests were the mediators and the only interpreters of the God's Law.

The New Testament church didn't pattern itself after the Jewish temple. Jesus never taught believers to be Levitical priests. Instead, Jesus taught these leaders to be servants. The disciples were cautioned not to be called rabbi or teacher (Mt.23:8-11). Christ, THE high priest (Heb. 3:1, 7:24), brought an end to daily animal sacrifice; for He completed the sacrifice. The Aaronic (Levitical) priesthood was no longer needed.

The Old Testament idea of the priest being the mediator between God and man was only necessary until the death of Jesus Christ. Now, Christ, our High Priest has the ministry of mediation (Heb. 7:25) and He gives us all the right to be priests after His nature.

Jesus never appointed or designated His apostles to return to the OLD priesthood type of function. Jesus brought forth a brand new priesthood of believers. Jesus instituted a kingdom of priests all tribes and people, and every believer. Jesus is a priest after the order of Melchezedek and He has given that priesthood to all of us.

What do king/priests after the order of Melchizedek actually do?

Priests primarily offer up prayers and supplications to God, and kings, by their God given authority, decree God's will in the earth.

That means that the priestly ministry is one of drawing close to the Father through worship, priestly intercession, and prayer, and in so doing one can discern the heart and mind of God. In doing that, one can then, by means of kingly decree, speak forth the will of the Father into a situation in the earth as a prophetic proclamation, and by doing that heaven comes to earth!

Every believer in this royal priesthood is called to prayer, worship, intercession, and praise. As believers, we are all God's priests through the blood of Jesus having access to the throne of grace. All believers are called to take up a position of worship and intercession before the throne of God. Hebrews13:15 says, *"Through Him, therefore, let us constantly and at all times offer up to God a sacrifice of praise, which is the fruit of lips that thankfully acknowledge and confess and glorify His name."*

We have been raised to sit with Jesus in heavenly places and thus are given access to God's Throne. Our prayers according to God's will shall reach His Throne and find approval leading to the release of power. *Raised us up together, and made us sit together in the heavenly places in Christ... Eph. 2:6.*

There are definite parallels between the duties of the Old Testament priests who served in the tabernacle of Moses and the priestly ministry of believers today. The functions of the Old Testament priests foreshadow the greater reality, God longs to see manifested in His priestly people today. "God intended all along to form for Himself a Kingdom of priests. He longs to call us closer, beyond the veil of separation, so He can meet and commune with us in the Most Holy Place of His manifest Presence.

Every New Testament priest of God is called and anointed to pray and intercede. A priest who does not pray isn't a priest at all! We as priest are called to enforce Jesus' authority on earth as His body.

God has chosen to raise up an entire Kingdom of priests and wants us to model our priesthood after the continual ministry of our Great High Priest, Jesus Christ.

The priestly ministry equips and enables us to affect the heavenly realm through worship, intimacy and our relationship with the Lord.

This allows us to enter His sanctuary and draw near to Him by offering the sacrifices of praise, worship, intercession and mutual exchange.

Prayer and worship were at the core of the daily activities of the first church. They met together in the temple courts as well as their homes daily. The first believers who were mostly Jews continued with the Jewish practice of daily prayer and worship at the temple. The key watch times in the temple during that time would have been 9:00 am, and 3:00 pm. In addition to these watches, the early church clearly had no problem with praying all night. This implies that worship, prayer and intercession should be the primary and foundation of ministry for every believer.

It is the strategy of Heaven to identify gates and appoint overseers with spiritual authority. This is applied both individually and corporately. We can individually bring forth from the Kingdom revelations of truth that are foundational and at the same time fresh and unprecedented.

This revelation that will be delegated from the Kingdom of God will be both new and old. We will not only bring forward the delegation of truth imparted to prior generations, but we will also release the mysteries and secrets set apart for this age.

Jesus said to his disciples, *"Truly, truly, I say to you, he who believes in Me, the works that I do, he will do also; and greater works than these he will do; because I go to the Father." John 14:12.* These will be the sons of the Kingdom who carry the Sevenfold Spirit of God that rested upon the Lord Himself.

Kingdom Keys

"I will give you the keys of the kingdom of heaven; and whatever you bind on earth shall have been bound in heaven, and whatever you loose on earth shall have been loosed in heaven." Mt 16:19

In dealing with the Kingdom there are a number of things that we must first grasp in terms of the Kingdom. The Kingdom of God manifests itself in various levels. Life is lived on levels and experienced in stages established on dimensions. So as we begin to aspire to understand the Kingdom, please know that there are agencies in the earth that have been designed to keep us out of the Kingdom of God.

The Bible says that the god of this world has blinded the minds of individuals so that they don't access the Kingdom of God. *In whom the god of this world hath blinded the minds of them which believe not, lest the light of the glorious gospel of Christ, who is the image of God, should shine unto them. 2 Cor.4:4*

For us to have access to the Kingdom we have to have certain keys to get in.

The Bible uses a key as a symbol of authority. In Isaiah 22:22, we see Eliakim the priest receiving "the key of the house of David...on his shoulder." Revelation 3:7 uses similar symbolism. A trusted servant to the king wore the key to the king's house on a hook on his shoulder. Therefore, he had the authority to open or close the king's house.

Anciently, when one came to seek the king's help or counsel, the servant's job was to open the door to the king's house and assist him in reaching the king. We as Christians, have a similar responsibility to assist those whom God is calling.

When God puts these keys in our hands, they grant us access into a greater dimension in the spirit realm.

Christ showed that the religious teachers of His day, who had access to the knowledge of God's ways, had failed in this duty. "Woe to you lawyers! For you have taken away the key of knowledge. You did not enter in yourselves, and those who were entering in you hindered" *(Luke 11:52).*

Having the keys is not a matter of controlling access to the kingdom, as is often thought. Keys do not first mean the right to control access, but the enjoyment of access. Imagine a man who carefully kept his doors locked and his keys in hand, but never went into his house! Having access to the kingdom isn't our ultimate goal, living in it, is what matters.

Occasionally, the ministry has the sad duty to inform some that because of their choices and actions, the doors to the kingdom are being closed to them unless they repent. See 1 Corinthians 5 or 2 Thessalonians 3:14

The Lord must be able to trust us with the use of the *"Keys of the Kingdom."* We need to simply understand that our confidence in Jesus as the one who "has say over all things in heaven and in earth" *(Matt. 28:18)* can develop into practical access to the riches of the Kingdom.

We are improving the world of our day and time.

When Jesus comes to walk with us in our present environment, He should find pleasure and satisfaction in what we have accomplished, because we have been given the keys that will unlock and release the enemy's grip on the governments that rule the nations.

The Watchmen

The Hebrew term "Shamar" is frequently used throughout Scripture and is the term used in Genesis 2:15 *"Then the Lord God took the man and put him in the garden of Eden to tend (watch) and keep it."* The term to *"tend* and *keep*" is "S*hamar*" often used for the term "*watch*" biblically. To watch is God's first command to man as He created Him. We are therefore all called to "*watch*."

Let's look at "*watch*."

The word "*watch*", in Scripture, signifies a division of the night. Additionally, to watch means to look out, to peer into the distance, to investigate or get a new scope on something to see an approaching danger, and warn those endangered. To watch also means to review and evaluate your household or to see so you can guard your future.

Several words linked with watching are: shaqad (to "be alert") - to be wakeful, so you can see either for good or evil *(Jeremiah 31:28; 51:12, Isaiah 29:20);* shamar (to "protect") - may mean a day or night watch; thus, there was a guard of the king's house *(2 Kings 11:5-7,*

Nehemiah 4:9; 7:3); gregoreo (to "keep awake, to watch") - to take heed, lest through remissiveness and indolence one be led to forsake Christ *(Matthew 26:41; Mark 14:38);* nepho (to "abstain from wine, be sober") - used in the NT figuratively, to be calm and collected in spirit; to be temperate, dispassionate, circumspect *(1 Thessalonians 5:6; 2 Timothy 4:5).*

Let's look at how "watchman" was used in scripture.

Now David was sitting between the two gates. And the <u>watchman</u> went up to the roof over the gate, to the wall, lifted his eyes and looked, and there was a man, running alone. Then the <u>watchman</u> cried out and told the king. And the king said, "If he is alone, there is news in his mouth." And he came rapidly and drew near. Then the <u>watchman</u> saw another man running, and the <u>watchman</u> called to the gatekeeper and said, "There is another man, running alone!" And the king said, "He also brings news." So the <u>watchman</u> said, "I think the running of the first is like the running of Ahimaaz the son of Zadok." And the king said, "He is a good man, and comes with good news." (2 Samuel 18:24 -27)

Now a <u>watchman</u> stood on the tower in Jezreel, and he saw the company of Jehu as he came, and said, "I see a company of men." And Joram said, "Get a horseman, and send him to meet them, and let him say, 'Is it peace?'" (II Kings 9:17)

For thus has the Lord said to me: "Go, set a <u>watchman</u>, let him declare what he sees." (Isaiah 21:6)

"Son of man, speak to the children of your people, and say to them: 'When I bring the sword upon a land, and the people of the land take a man from their territory and make him their <u>watchman</u>, 'when he sees the sword coming upon the land, if he blows the trumpet and warns the people, 'then whoever hears the sound of the trumpet and does not take warning, if the sword comes and takes him away, his blood shall be on his own head.... ......'But if the <u>watchman</u> sees the sword coming and does not blow the trumpet, and the people are not warned, and the sword comes and takes any person from among them, he is taken away in his iniquity; but his blood I will require at the <u>watchman's</u> hand.' "So you, son of man: I have made you a <u>watchman</u> for the house of Israel; therefore you shall hear a word from My mouth and warn them for Me. (Ez.33:2-7)

In looking through these portions of scripture we learn a number of things about watchmen.

- First, the watchman can be stationed in a number of places but is often by a gate on a wall.

- Second, the watchman simply reports what he sees and hears to the kings or elders who sit in the gates. The authority in the gate makes the decisions as to what actions should be taken and gives orders.

- Third, as long as the watchman is reporting all that he has seen and all that he has heard, he is fulfilling his responsibility.

Nevertheless we made our prayer to our God, and because of them we set a watch against them day and night. (Neh 4:9)

To Shuppim and Hosah the lot came out for the West Gate, with the Shallecheth Gate on the ascending highway–watchman opposite watchman. (1Chr 26:16)

And the heads of the Levites were Hashabiah, Sherebiah, and Jeshua the son of Kadmiel, with their brothers across from them, to praise and give thanks, group alternating with group, according to the command of David the man of God. (Neh 12:24)

Mattaniah, Bakbukiah, Obadiah, Meshullam, Talmon, and Akkub were gatekeepers keeping the watch at the storerooms of the gates.(Neh 12:25)

We see in the preceding scriptures that the watch is filled by someone performing the function of a watchman. Their job is to watch over all that is in their view and to report what they see and hear. They can be assigned on the wall, by a gate, during the day, during the night, by a storeroom, it can be a priestly function and they are under command.

I will stand my watch and set myself on the rampart, and watch to see what He will say to me, and what I will answer when I am corrected. Then the LORD answered me and said: "Write the vision and make it plain on tablets, that he may run who reads it. (Hab 2:1-2)

In **Psalm 5:3** the term "I will look up" is the term for watchman and in **Habukuk 2:1-2** speaks of being a watchman before the Lord, reporting what you see or hear and writing it down. In other words, there is a place to set watchmen before the Lord to see what He would say to us so we can get direction and strategy and we should record this information.

In Nelson's Bible Dictionary we learn that a watch is a group of soldiers or others posted to keep guard. It also refers to one of the units of time into which a night watch was divided *(Ps. 63:6, Lam. 2:19, Luke 12:38)*.

In the Old Testament we learn that there must have been 3 such watches because of the term "middle watch" in *Judges 7:19*

Ex.14:24, and *1 Sam. 11:11* speaks of "morning watch".

However, in the New Testament period the Roman system of 4 watches was adopted. *Mark 6:48; Matt. 14:25*

We also learn from Nelson's Bible Dictionary that a "watchtower" was an observation tower upon which a guard or lookout was stationed to keep watch. This was an elevated platform *(2 Kings 17:9, 18:8, Isa. 21:8)*. We also learn from Nelson's about the purpose of a tower. A tower was a tall building erected for defense. Some landowners used towers to protect their crops *(Isa. 5:2, Matt.21:33, Mark 12:1)*. In the wilderness, towers were used to watch for approaching marauders *(2 Kings 17:9, 2 Chr. 26:10)*. In cities towers was part of the walls built for defensive purposes *(2 Chr. 14:7, Neh. 3:1)*. They were erected at the corners of the wall, beside the city gates, and at intervals along the walls *(2 Chr. 26:9)*. Watchmen secured the towers *(2 Kings 9:17)* and arrow and stone throwing machines were mounted on the towers *(2 Chr. 26:15)*.

In *Ezekiel 3:17* we see the prophet Ezekiel is referred to as a watchman for the nation of Israel. In *Ezekiel 33:1-7* we learn of some of the responsibility of the watchmen. They are to warn the people when they see danger approaching. As long as they report what they see and hear then they have fulfilled their responsibility.

So what can we learn from all of this information?

- Watchmen simply report what they see and hear. Watchmen report the approach of an enemy or the approach of the king.
- They report to the authorities who sit in the gates.
- They are usually stationed at every gate and along the walls at various points. However, they can be stationed other places as well.
- They are under command.

- Though a watchman is usually a soldier, they do not attack without specific orders. Their primary function is to report what they see and hear.
- Their post is often in a watchtower, an elevated structure specially fortified for that purpose. The position is one of a defense. Though siege weapons could be mounted and operated from the tower platform.
- There is no place in the Bible that indicates a watchman went out and attacked an army. They simply reported what they saw and heard and obeyed the commands of those in authority. The king or commanding officer might send out an army to attack, but the watchman did not give such an order. (Note: the prophet Ezekiel in Ezekiel 3 was referred to as a watchman and in Jeremiah the prophet in Jeremiah 1:10 was to root out, pull down, destroy and throw down, build and plant. Hence, it is possible for those with a prophetic gifting functioning as watchmen to at some point function as the prophet did in Jeremiah)
- The watchmen were usually soldiers and often carried weapons. It was

permissible to use these in extreme cases such as self-defense.

- There was often a captain of the guard or watch whom the watchmen reported to and who prepared reports for the leaders. (Nehemiah 7:2 –Hanani was leader of the citadel or captain of the guard)

Watchmen are to WATCH and PRAY and REPORT ALL THAT THEY SEE AND HEAR. A watchman will not always understand all that he hears or sees, but that is OK. Their job is just to report what they see and hear.

Prayer Watches are to:

- promote intimacy with God
- protect defensively and offensively
- help establish government
- pave the way for the future

A Time to Watch

There is an appointed time for everything. And there is a time for every event under heaven—Eccl. 3:1

Anciently, the division of the day was into three parts, namely, the morning-the heat of the day, commencing about the middle of the forenoon-midday, and evening. In a similar manner, the Greeks appear at first to have divided the night also into three parts or watches, namely, the first watch, the middle, or second watch, and the morning, or third watch. But after the Jews became subject to the Romans, they adopted the Roman manner of dividing the night into four watches, namely, the evening, or first quarter, after sunset; the midnight; cock-crowing, or third quarter, from midnight on; and the morning, or fourth quarter, including the dawn.

To begin with, God does everything for a reason, because He is a God of purpose. His actions are not arbitrary. *The Lord Almighty has sworn, Surely, as I have planned, so it will be, and as I have purposed, so it will stand. (Isa. 14:24.) The plans of the Lord stand firm forever, the purposes of his heart through all generations. (Ps. 33:11) Many are the plans in a man's heart, but it is the Lord's purpose that prevails. (Prov. 19:21)*

How important is it that we "watch"? Consider this: the bible commands us to watch and pray.

Let's look at Jesus' warning to "watch". Just what did He mean?

Jesus said to his disciples the following:

Matthew 24:"Watch out that no one deceives you" (verse 4); "See to it that you are not alarmed" (verse 6); "Stand firm to the end" (verse 13); "Keep watch" (verse 42). In Mark 13: "Watch out that no one deceives you" (verse 5); "Do not be alarmed" (verse 7); "Be on your guard" (verse 9); "Do not worry" (verse 11); "Stand firm" (verse 13); "Be on your guard" (verse 23); "Be on your guard. Be alert" (verse 33); "Keep watch" (verse 35); "Watch out" (verse 37). And in Luke 21: "Watch out that you are not deceived" (verse 8); "Do not be frightened" (verse 9); "Stand firm" (verse 19); "Stand up and lift up your heads" (verse 28); "Be careful" (verse 34).; "Be always on the watch and pray" (verse 36).

Significantly, the very first thing that Jesus responded with was a warning of what to watch out for: *"Take heed that no one deceives you."* Watching helps our praying, and praying helps our watching.

Peter warns us, *"Be sober, be vigilant, because your adversary the devil walks about like a roaring lion, seeking whom he may devour" (1 Peter 5:8).* Staying aware of the behind-the-scenes role of Satan and his demons enables us to understand what's really going on in the spirit. It also enables us to *"resist"* them *(James 4:7)*.

The attributes of the spiritual atmosphere surrounding a region dictates the characteristics that region demonstrates. For instance, if spirits of witchcraft and sorcery predominantly occupy the heavenly places over a region then many of the people living under that jurisdiction will be captured by these spirits. Likewise, if an open Heaven can be achieved over a territory, then righteousness and truth will flourish. Many souls will be won through a fruitful harvest and God's people will walk with Him in fellowship.

James 5:16, we are told that the effectual fervent prayers of a righteous man availeth much. As we pray, we stand watch over our families, cities, and nations. Just as men stood on city walls in the Bible to watch for approaching danger, God calls us to be modern-day watchmen and warn those who are endangered *(2 Kings 9:17-18)*.

We are to watch not only for the enemy's activity but also for the manifestation of God's plans. If we watch for the enemy and announce his activity, we can avert the devil's plans to steal, kill and destroy what God has for us. Jesus said in *Matthew 24:43, "But know this, if the good man of the house had known in what watch the thief would come, he would have watched and would not have suffered his house to be broken up."*

The Lord is stretching forth His hand to fill our mouths with decrees and proclamations from his heart. The anointed words of God's people will uproot the forces of darkness and plant the revelation of His Kingdom. When this takes place there will be an abundant harvest of souls and the Lord Jesus will begin to receive the full measure of His great reward. *(Revelations 5:9)*

We are presently living in a season of spiritual breakthrough. The Heavenly host has been assigned to us in this task. Our responsibility is to articulate the Lord's desires through the revelation of His Kingdom. The battle is won in the Spirit first then manifested in the natural. This is our strategy for corporate breakthrough. *Wherefore comfort one another with these words. But concerning the times and the seasons, brethren, ye have no need that aught be written unto you. For yourselves know perfectly that the day of the Lord so cometh as a thief in the night. 1 Thess. 4:18-5:2*

Prayer moves the hands of God. Even as He spoke the universe into creation, God created us in His image. Our spoken words and prayers carry the power of creation within them. As intercessors and God's watchmen on the walls of our families, cities and nations, we are called to watch over our assignments to see approaching danger and warn those endangered. *(2Kings 9:17, 18)*

THE EARLY NIGHT WATCH OR FIRST WATCH OF THE NIGHT

(6.00 PM – 9.00 PM)

The First (Evening) Watch is from 6:00 p.m. – 9:00 p.m. The Israelites ordered their prayer times accordingly, beginning with 6:00 p.m. – 9:00 p.m. which is a time of quiet reflection. Jesus used the evening watch to go aside and pray. *(Matt. 14:15-23)* In the early church, this watch at sundown was a time of corporate prayer (Vespers) where candles were lit, Psalms sung, thanksgiving offered, prayers said and blessings invoked. After the business of the day, it is a time to release anxieties to the Lord before sleep. During this watch, ask God to give you clear directions for the day ahead and about His call on your life.

Silence all the Voices (Curses) of the Enemies on our life and family.

During this watch the struggle that is taking place is a spiritual confrontation in heavenly places *(Eph 6:12).*

People involved in the occult say that they begin their active witchcraft at midnight. They say that during this time witches start flying around the precincts of the city because they intend to take hold of the gates of the day. *They return at evening, they howl like a dog, And go around the city. Ps 59:6* I like how Adam Clark Commentary articulates the above scripture. It reads: *"When the beasts of prey leave their dens, and go prowling about the cities and villages to get offal, and entrap domestic animals, these come about the city to see if they may get an entrance, destroy the work, and those engaged in it".* If we begin to pray strategically during this watch with the Holy Spirit's leading, we can prevent the kingdom of darkness from releasing curses on the new day. We must possess the gate of our new day. Otherwise it will be the enemies possessing them.

God's decrees are issued to pluck up and overthrow things contrary to His kingdom. Likewise, commands are dispensed to also build and plant according to the Kingdom of God. *I, the Son of Man, will send my angels, and they will remove from my Kingdom everything that causes sin and all who do evil, Matthew 13:41.*

In Heaven, spiritual beings identified as messengers operate closely with us in Heaven. The messengers function in cooperation with God's people to see

Heavenly mandates and decrees accomplished. They can bring judgment or blessing from God's throne. It is the revelation of Heavenly justice. They record the desire of God and work with us for its fulfillment. God is sending messengers to co-labor with us, to pluck up and gather out of His Kingdom all stumbling blocks.

Covenant Renewal with God.

It was the watch during which Jesus broke bread and gave thanks to God. Through Jesus Christ, we have a Covenant with God. In this watch, we can appropriate the blessings of God's Covenant and ask Him to manifest those blessing into our lives. Every covenant you have with God can be renewed at this time.

Humility Check

Humility is the greatest secret of His strength: that is the reason why during this watch, He tied the towel around His waist and washed His disciples' feet. Leadership is service.

Therefore, we are to pray:

- I now pray with all prayer and supplication in the Spirit, and I watch thereunto with all perseverance and supplication for all saints; *(Eph 6:13-18)*

- Spirit of Truth, I ask that you will bring the conviction of sin that initiates repentance. *(John 16:8-9)*

- I confess my sins, You Father are faithful and just to forgive and cleanse me. *(1 John 1:9)*

- I take dominion and nullify all the curses that the enemies have released on this new day.

- I clothe myself in humility *(1 Peter 5:5)*

- I declare and decree that the spirit of wisdom, understanding, divine counsel, supernatural might, knowledge and the fear of the Lord is upon me, and as I advance I am divinely empowered and increase in skill and understanding.

- I bind the accuser of the brethren from operating or influencing my mind.

- I place upon me the full armor and decree that the weapons of my warfare are not carnal, but mighty through God.

- In Jesus name, I pull down strongholds, cast down vain imaginations and every high thing that exalteth itself against the knowledge of God.

- I speak that God's anointing destroys every yoke and I invoke order according to God's divine systems.

- I now stand therefore, having my loins girt about with truth, and having on the breastplate of righteousness;

- My feet are shod with the preparation of the gospel of peace;

- I take the shield of faith, and I quench all the fiery darts of the wicked.

- I take the helmet of salvation, and the sword of the Spirit, which is the word of God:

- Holy Spirit, enlighten my spiritual eyes and give me access to the spiritual gates as established by the enemy in the land. *(Eph. 1:17-19; Matt. 16:18-19)*

- Father, release Your messengers to bring and then to see the Heavenly mandates and decrees accomplished. Let them bring judgment or blessing from Your throne.

- Father come *(Ps. 45:4; Ps. 74:12; Isa. 19:1)* and take hold of the gates of the nation and by the working of Your mighty strength and paralyze all the strongholds of the devil, so Jesus will be enthroned.

- Allow Your angels to operate the gates and release godliness and righteousness into my life, city, and this nation. *(Rev. 3:7, 20; Isa. 22:20-25, 26:2,3).*

- I cripple all the effects of the satanic prophets and priests in the land.

- I decree for the night to come over their eyes so their vision and declarations will be futile.

- I declare the judgment of the LORD upon the spirits of wickedness in the land. *(Isa. 17:12-14)*

- I decree and declare that a prayer shield, the anointing and bloodline form a hedge of protection which, hides me from all familiar spirits and all other demonic personalities, making it difficult for them to effectively track or trace me in the realm of the spirit. There shall be no penetrations.

- Send forth Your angels to arrest wicked spirits out to devastate the land and the people. I Invite You Lord into this nation, government, and this economy etc.

- Father come to town in Your glory so all the powers; principalities and wicked spirits that torment the people will be chased out of town.

- Father in Your judgment strike all the thrones of iniquity in my bloodline and let them be cut off. *(Ps 94:20; Ex 12:29)*

- Father extend Your right hand and come to the defense of the poor and the needy.

- I bind every hindrance and blockage to spiritual dreams and visitations.

- Father loose Your angels to come and guard my house and guard my night watch.

- I decree that I will have spiritual dreams!

- Father loose Your angels to come and visit me with revelation, understanding, wisdom, breakthrough, healing, deliverance, and every "good and perfect gift that comes from above" *(James 1:17)*

- Father release clear discernment during the night watch.

- Sing songs and give thanks to the Lord for securing our victory! (*1 Chr.23:30*)

- I appropriate the blessings of Jesus's Covenant and ask Father that You would allow them to manifest into our lives.

LATE NIGHT WATCH OR SECOND WATCH OF THE NIGHT

(9.00 PM – 12 Midnight)

Ps. 119:62 says, "At midnight I will rise to give thanks to You because of Your righteous judgments."

It was at the midnight hour that God struck down the first-born of Egypt, and, consequently, His people were released from captivity and set free to worship Him. This watch is a time when God deals with the enemies that are trying to keep us from entering into His perfect plan for our lives. In the natural, this time is characterized by deep darkness. In the spiritual realm, the Second Watch is when diabolical assignments and sabotage are set in motion as supernatural creatures, including witches and demons and practices like black magic, collaborate to effect change and transformation for the evil one. It is important for intercessors at this watch to give thanks for the protection of the shadow of God's wing and pray for a visitation from the Lord. "Let God arise and His enemies be scattered.

During this watch, intercessors are able to impact the spiritual realm before the enemy gets ready to wreak havoc.

Time for Divine Favor

This is the time to receive your provision or supply (strength, abilities, freedom from all limitations, etc.). This is also the time for plundering your oppressors. This is the time for favor from men.

Exodus 3:21- 22; 11:3-4; 12:35-36; you will see that God made the Egyptians favorably disposed towards the Israelites and they received whatever they asked for. This had to be done before midnight because it was at midnight that the angel of death passed through Egypt and no one could go on to the neighbors. It also had to be after supper, since it was after the Passover feast. Automatically it had to be during this watch of the night between 9.00pm and 12.00 midnight.

In *Acts 23:23* we see Paul enjoying favor from the captain of the soldiers during this same period.
It is the time to pray for the release or outpouring of the Spirit of Grace, of Prayer and Supplication.

Let's look at the meanings of supplication and petition:

- Supplication: Entreaty; humble and earnest prayer in worship. In all our supplications to the Father of mercies, let us remember a world lying in ignorance and wickedness.
- Petition: earnest request; In Roman times, it consisted in sacrifices, feasting, offering thanks, and praying for a continuance of success.

Grace is defined as; unmerited help given to people by God. Freedom from sin through divine grace; A virtue coming from God; Approval; acceptance; Ease of movement; honor; adorn; embellish

(Matt. 26:36-46) Recall that on the day Jesus was betrayed, He started praying for God's grace at 9.00 pm. At 10.00 pm, He came back to His disciples and said, "Could you not watch with me one hour?" At 11.00 pm, He came a second time and said "Are you still sleeping?" He left them and went back. Then the third time that was 12 midnight, He said, "Rise, and let us go for my betrayer is at hand." This period is the time to pray for strength against all temptation and trials.

Time for Divine Protection

This is also the period to pray and ask for the release of the troops of God to be on patrol and give angelic escort *(Zech. 1:10, Acts 9:23)*. *Acts 23:23*, the same army General that had arrested Paul, now ended up protecting Paul! As you pray today, God would cause the people who have arrested us before to protect His purpose for our lives. What the governor could not enjoy was given to Paul as he was given 470 soldiers as escort. So every provision we need to do God's work would be released at this time. That is why even in Hollywood this is the time they show all the bad films to make provision for your being affected in the next watch.

Time for Provisions

Time for the supply of resources needed for every God-given project – see *Ex. 35* and *36* also look at *Ex.12:35, 36*. It was the time that the Israelites got everything that they had to use to build the Tabernacle in the wilderness. This is also the time to ask for the sense of urgency to accomplish whatever God wants us to do. The Israelites ate the Passover standing with their tunics tucked with belts around their waists ready to move!

Therefore, we are to pray:

- In Jesus Name, I declare and decree God's original plans and purposes over and against the plans and purposes of Satan.

- I decree and declare that no weapon, be it emotional, financial, physical, social, spiritual, psychological, organizational, interpersonal, formed against me shall prosper, and every tongue that shall rise up against me is condemned

- I command every evil sanction, corrupt activity, and satanic order, which opposes the will of the Lord concerning my life be destroyed.

- I disannul every evil decision and ruling concerning my life, family, ministry, and anyone associated to me.

- Father, I ask that You release the angels assigned to me to handle any satanic contentions, disputing's, strivings and resistance concerning this order.

- I bind any further demonic movements and satanic activities emanating from the underworld against me.

- I reverse the effect of any stigmas and declare and decree that divine favor, grace, honor and well wishes now replace any and all negative feelings, perceptions and thoughts concerning me, the ministry and anything I am called to accomplish.

- I bind and cast out every lying spirit, gossip, slander, backbiting, disloyalty, waywardness, wandering and every negative spirit and I bind my heart, mind and spirit to the mind of God and the Holy Spirit, in the name of Jesus.

- I declare and decree that nobility and greatness is my portion.

- I bind all oppressors so that my house lacks no good thing.

- I will not miss my hour of favor when it comes *(Ex. 3:22).*

- I loose every limitation of my gifts and abilities.

- I declare my days of sorrow come to an end *(Is. 60:20).*

- Lord make my enemies favorably disposed towards me so much so that their own testimony of me will extend tremendous goodwill towards You *(Ex. 3:21).*

- Father release Your favor, protection and preservation into the foundations of my family, community and the church as a whole *(Acts 23:23-31; Esther 2:9).*

- Father release the Spirit of Grace & Supplication upon me to overcome temptations and trials.

- Father release the Supply of all Resources needed for every God-given project – *(see Ex. 35 and 36 also look at Ex.12:35, 36.)*

- Give me the unction down in my spirit Lord to accomplish whatever You want me to do. *(The Israelites ate the Passover standing with their tunics tucked with belts around their waists ready to move!)*

- This is my set time for favor. *Psalm 102:13*

- Lord, I entreat Your favor. *Psalm 45:12*

- Be favorable unto my land, and let my horn be exalted. *Psalm 85:1; 89:17*

- Lord, I entreat Your favor with my whole heart. *Psalm 119:58*

- Let Your favor be upon my life as a cloud of the latter rain. *Proverbs 16:15*

- Let Your beauty be upon my life and let me be well favored. *Genesis 29:17*

- Lord, I know You favor me, because my enemies do not triumph over me. *Psalm 41:11*

- Let me be satisfied with favor, and filled with Your blessing. *Deuteronomy 33:23*

- Lord, bless my latter end more than my beginning. *Job 42:12*

- Thank You for Your mercies that are new every morning; You daily load me with benefits. *Lamentations 3:23; Psalm 68:19*

- By Your favor, Lord, let my mountain stand strong. *Psalm 30:7*

- Lord, bless me, and cause Your face to shine upon me, that Your way may be known upon the earth and Your saving health among all nations. Let my land yield its increase, its harvest, its blessing, and let the ends of the earth fear You. *Psalm 67*

THE MIDNIGHT WATCH OR THIRD WATCH OF THE NIGHT

(12.00 AM – 3.00 AM)

This is a period of much spiritual activity. This watch is the darkest and most demonic part of the night, especially at midnight. Witches, warlocks, and Satanists have fun and start their incantations during this part of the night.

Satan is neither omnipotent nor omnipresent; therefore, he works through a host of unclean spirits. These unclean spirits comes to influence, manipulate, and control the structural powers. When these unclean spirits are dispersed into the world, they bring confusion and chaos.

It is their mission to try and stop any potential threat to their control. Ultimately their goal is to produce evil, oppression, and rebellion against God.

They are divided based on geopolitical, geographical, and territories that cover the entire world. *For we wrestle not against flesh and blood, but against principalities, against powers, against the rulers of the darkness of this world, against spiritual wickedness in high places (Eph. 6:12)*

This is a powerful watch to be on when commanding the morning and setting things in place before the devil and his demons have a chance to ruin it. Plane crashes, car crashes, deaths, job loss, and many other acts of the devil can be stopped during this watch when intercessors obey the voice of the Lord and saturate this time with powerful Spirit-led prayers.

Time for Spiritual Warfare

This is a time for divine government to overrule human decrees! *(Ex. 12 – 14)*. This is when the deep sleep falls upon men according to *Acts 20:7-12*. Remember, according to *Matt. 13:25*, while men slept the enemy went to sow tares. The enemy knows that there are not many people praying to oppose him. *(Matt. 13:24; 1 King 3:20)* This watch is the weak link for Islam – only a few Sufis are praying at this time!!! The story is different during the month of Ramadan when every Muslim is encouraged to pray the "Tahajjud."

It is also the time for slaying; when the destroying angel goes through the camp, neighborhood, community, city, or nation *(Ex. 12:29; 2Kings 19:35)*. Time to declare *Psalm 91:5, 6* for Divine Protection for yourself, family, church, city and nation. This period is also the time that rapists increase their activity, according to *Judges 19*, the Levite's concubine was raped about this period and was only left to go before dawn, so pray and silence them *(Judges 19:25)*.

Often we are awakened during this time with dreams God has given to us. God uses dreams and visions to bring instruction and counsel to us as we sleep and reveals areas where we need to concentrate our prayers and intercession. *(Judges 16:2, 3; Job 33:15)* The devil can also attack you in dreams (nightmares), so always pray before you go to sleep and ask God to keep you from the enemy's devices.

This watch hour will strengthen your faith. It is a time to pray to fortify yourself against doubt and unbelief and even the direction of your path. Be vigilant during this time and watch for God's revelation for breakthrough for His plans and purposes for your life and territory.

Time of Release from Prison (I really love this part!) ☺

Paul and Silas were released from prison during this time *(Acts 16:25)*. Samson escaped from Gaza at midnight by pulling up the gates of the city and carrying them out with him *(Judges 16:3-4).* In addition, God released the people of Israel from Egypt at this time *(Exodus 12:31).* This is the time for angelic intervention!

This is the period to pray for God's provision to be released *(Luke 11:5-13; Acts 16:3).* It is the time for miracles and for applying the Blood of Jesus.

This is the time the wicked are wiped out. In *2 Kings 19* Hezekiah is greatly distressed, and sends to Isaiah to pray for him. Isaiah returns and predicts the destruction of the king of Assyria and his army. Sennacherib, hearing that his kingdom was invaded by the Ethiopians, sends a terrible letter to Hezekiah telling him to surrender. Hezekiah goes to the temple, spreads the letter before the Lord, and prays. Isaiah is sent to him to assure him that his prayer is heard and that Jerusalem will be delivered and that the Assyrians will be destroyed. That very night a messenger of God slays one hundred and eighty-five thousand Assyrians. Sennacherib returns to Nineveh, and is slain by his own sons. *Then it happened that night that the angel of the LORD went out and struck 185,000 in the camp of the Assyrians; and when men rose early in the morning, behold, all of them were dead. 2 Kings 19:35*

At evening time, behold, there is terror! Before morning they are no more. Such will be the portion of those who plunder us And the lot of those who pillage us. Isa. 17:14.

FREEDOM of Bride

This is the time to pray for the freedom of the bride, especially those who are trusting God for their marriage partners. For those who are married, this probably the best time to pray for your marriage. According to *Matt. 25:6,* it was at midnight that the Bridegroom came.

In the case of Ruth, though she had been sleeping at Boaz's feet, it was at midnight that he noticed that a woman was sleeping there. Pray for God to show you things to make your marriage a happy one *(Ruth 3:1-10).* Pray also for the discovery of new and beautiful things in your spouse. This period is also the time to keep the lamps burning *(Matt. 25:5-10).* This watch is the time to enter your rest *(Ps. 67).*

Make your case

How hopeless we would be if in the darkness of sin there was no friend to go to for help and relief. However, it is good to know that in the blackness of whatever midnight we may face, there is a Friend who will rise up and bless us.

Abraham pleaded for Sodom. *Abraham approached him and said, "Will you destroy both innocent and guilty alike? Genesis 18:23.* Jacob wrestled with the angel of the covenant. *"Your name will no longer be Jacob," the man told him. "It is now Israel, because you have struggled with both God and men and have won." Genesis 32:28.*

The Syro-Phoenician woman pleaded on behalf of her daughter *Matthew 15:21-28.* WHY did God honor such persistence, and by this parable command us to emulate it? He is PLEASED with it!" Let men pray ALWAYS. This is the period to pray for every emergency provision to be released.

Therefore, we are to pray:
- Father, in the name of Jesus, destroy the works of witches & warlocks who withstand the anointing as you did in the day of Moses. Confound the omens of the liars, astrologers, psychics, prognosticators, sorcerers, and the like.

Make fools of diviners and make their dark knowledge foolishness.

- I rebuke and dismantle satanic alliances and confederations. Father arrest them by the spirit.

- Let every covert effort fail.

- In Jesus Name I disappoint the devices the enemy has crafted, so that their hands cannot perform their enterprise.

- Father take them in their own crafty and devious ways, let them meet with darkness in the daytime, and grope in the noonday as in the night.

- I overthrow and sabotage every strategic setback by the blood of the Lamb.

- Let every attack of retaliation fail in Jesus Name.

- Father, I ask You to contend with those who contend with me, fight with those who fight with me. *(Isa. 49:25)*

- I bind all satanic activity set up as a decoy or an ambush for my life.

- Father, in Jesus Name, overthrow the plans of troublemakers, scorners, scoffers, mockers, persecutors, and character assassins.

- Expose satanic representatives and grant unto me divine strategies and tactics to identify, resist and overcome the plots and plans established for my demise.

- Be my shield and buckler and fight this battle for me.

- Let terror strike the hearts of my enemies and cause their hearts to fail. It is you Jesus that give me stability, you have equipped me with salvation, Your right hand establishes me as a victor in the battle.

- I bind all distractive, disturbing and destructive measures.

- Father, beat down my enemy, give me his neck, cause me to pursue and overtake them until they are wounded and consumed, falling at my feet, never to rise again.

- Establish my name in the Heaven. Let them that hear of me submit and obey.

- I bind all opposing activities of any satanic personalities with devilish assignments concerning my life and my family

- I bind any demonic interception and interference or resistance in Jesus Name.

- I resist satanic activity and negotiations concerning my life and my soul.

- I come against all activities and opposing forces that are contrary to the will of God in Jesus Christ.

- I bind satanic harassment and rebuke satanic concentrations, and prohibit all satanic surveillance. In Jesus Name

- I lift false burdens and remove feelings of heaviness, oppression and depression.

- I overrule and over throw according to *Isaiah 54:17* all ill spoken words, and demonic activity, prayers and every idle word spoken contrary to God's original plans and purposes.

- In Jesus name, I reverse any and all word curses and decree and declare that they shall not stand, they shall not come to pass, they shall not take root and their violent verbal dealings returns to them double fold.

- I declare and decree that every lying tongue is wrong and that the truth prevails.

- In Jesus name, I war for the releasing of finances and all resources that belong to me.

- Everything prepared for me before the foundation of the world, that pertains to my life (ministry, calling) and godliness comes to me now.

- I call in resources from the north, the south, the east and the west. I declare and decree that every recourse necessary for me to fulfill Your original plans and purposes comes to me without delay, NOW.

- I declare and decree that the wealth of the wicked is no longer laid up for me, but is released NOW into my hands. Let those who hold on to my wealth longer than they should, be afflicted and tormented without relief until they release what rightfully belongs to me.

- I command SATAN to loose all that he has stolen from me illegally sevenfold!!

- I come against the spirit of deprivation for the Lord prospers the work of my hands. By Him and through Him I will accomplish great exploits.

- I declare and decree success and progress in my life.

- I declare freedom for His Bride *(Ex. 12:29; Judges 19:25)*

- I break every spirit of Limitation that has been sitting on me. *(Ex. 4:22-23)*.

- Father May the light from Your presence dawn and consume every iota of darkness, so that my family can enjoy the free release of the Holy Spirit *(Acts 16:24-25)*.

THE DAWN OR EARLY MORNING WATCH

(3.00 AM-6.00 AM)

This fourth watch is always important because this is the last watch of the night. This watch is the time that the satanic agents who went out to perform their activities are returning to their bases.

This is time for deliverance according to *Exodus 12 and 14*. This is also the time Jesus walked on the water to release the disciples from the storms *(Matthew 14:25-33)*. This is the time to ask the new day to speak into your life according to God's will *(Psalm 19:2)*. Command your morning!

Matthew 24:43 says: *"But know this, that if the good man of the house had known in what watch the thief would come, he would have watched, and would not have suffered his house to be broken up."* This is a disciplined prayer watch for those who have the power and training to wake up early in the morning and set the atmosphere. This is the time for all of the enemy's plans and strategies to fail. This watch is for gaining territory, establishing the spirit of prosperity and stopping the devil from hijacking blessings and favor. This prayer watch sets our day before it begins.

Time for Divine Judgments

God permits us, on His behalf, to wield the scepter of righteousness, the scepter with the name of the Lord Jesus Christ written upon it. And as we wield that scepter, we cast down the scepter of wickedness, destroying the dominion of Satan. We move back into the area which God has allotted to us. There is a promise for God's people to regain their inheritance in Christ. "The scepter of wickedness shall not remain over the land allotted to the righteous."

Satan and his hordes are determined to stop us from entering into our destiny. Our spiritual enemy is throwing everything at us with the goal to discourage us, confuse us, and sow doubt and anxiety into our heart. His ultimate intentions are to stop us from believing God for our promises, to divert us from our calling, and to lead us to deviate from the place where God has promised to place us. Be Still and Know that God is in Full Control.

This watch is the time that those satanic agents who went out to perform their activities are returning back to their *home base* so that they are not caught. As soon as the light begins to dawn upon the earth, thieves, assassins, murderers, and adulterers, who all hate and shun the light, fly like ferocious beasts to their several dens and hiding places; for such do not dare to come to the light, lest their works be manifest. This is the period to release the manifestation of the full intensity of the dayspring shaking out the wicked.

Though some scholars believe the dayspring falls between 12 midnight stretching up to 6:00am, the full impact of its intensity is felt in the final watch of this period (3:00am – 6:00am) when it begins to shake everything out.

This explains why the agents of the kingdom of darkness: those linked with Satan, heighten their activities, especially between the hours of 12 midnight and 3.00am, knowing that by the next watch (3.00 am – 6.00 am) they'll have to cease their activities lest they be caught by the full intensity of the dayspring.

Testimonies of former witches converted to Christianity attest to this. They tell of experiences, where when they went out of their bodies on witchcraft operation, they had to return into their bodies before 6.00 am, otherwise they would not be able to. This is because they will have been shaken out by the dayspring in line with *Job 38:13*. No spirit is supposed to remain in this state by daybreak, we see this demonstrated by Jacob's encounter with the Angel of the Lord in *Gen. 32:24-30*.

Time for Resurrection Power

This is the time we have to pray that everything that has died in our lives to resurrect. (dreams, visions, promises, etc.) This is the time to rise and begin to shine. *Isa. 60:1-5.* Every redemptive gift is to rise and shine, that is why, immediately after this watch the sun rises, and shines. *For You light my lamp; The LORD my God illumines my darkness Ps. 18:28.*

This is the time the stone in front of the tomb of Jesus was rolled away. Every reproach must be rolled away. God says He has a covenant with the day and also with the night.

Resurrection power operates through love and it is a dying to self. It moves through humility. As we humble ourselves before God to the point of obedience we cooperate with the Holy Spirit's work of sanctification in us.

Obedience follows humility, *"He humbled Himself and became obedient to the point of death"* We also must empty ourselves through humility to the point of obedience.

You might ask, "How do I die to self?"

Obedience to the voice of God is in itself a form of dying to yourself; it is giving up your life with the result of experiencing God's life. Every time we deny ourselves, which is giving up our life, we receive more of His life in us. *Then Jesus said to His disciples, "If anyone desires to come after Me, let him deny himself, and take up his cross, and follow Me. For whoever desires to save his life will lose it, but whoever loses his life for My sake will find it (Matthew 16:24 – 25).*

Paul went down to the street to resurrect Eutychus from the dead. *Acts 20:8—10, "There were many lamps in the upper room where we were gathered together. And there was a young man named Eutychus sitting on the window sill, sinking into a deep sleep; and as Paul kept on talking, he was overcome by sleep and fell down from the third floor and was picked up dead. But Paul went down and fell upon him, and after embracing him, he said, 'Do not be troubled, for his life is in him.'"*

Paul humbled himself and went down into the street and released resurrection power and brought Eutychus back to life. We are called to do the same. *Matthew 10:8, "Heal the sick, raise the dead, cleanse the lepers, cast out demons. Freely you received, freely give."* When Paul humbled himself died to his ways, resurrection power was released. During this time of transitioning into the resurrection power, God is calling believers to love and pray as never before. We are to seek His face while He may be found. *Psalm 105:4—5, "Seek the Lord and His strength; seek His face continually. Remember His wonders which He has done, His marvels and the judgments uttered by His mouth."*

Therefore, we are to pray:

- I execute divine judgment against satanic/demonic activities and I war in the spirit of Elijah and Jehu.(come against the spirit of Jezebel and overcome and overthrow her)

- I nullify, dismantle, cancel any satanic operations which are designed to delay God's original plans and purposes from their quick, swift and speedy manifestation.

- I declare and decree this day that I will operate according to God's divine will.

- I decree that God's agenda is my agenda. I submit to God and God alone.

- I bind all abortive measures, strategies and tactics of the enemy.

- Father let the light of Jesus expose every darkness and den of wickedness in my family, ministry, city, and nation. Uproot them and replace them with the light of his countenance. *And there is no creature hidden from His sight, but all things are open and laid bare to the eyes of Him with whom we have to do. Heb. 4:13.*

- By a strong east wind drive away all the darkness that has surrounded my family.

- Father may Your scepter of righteousness be witnessed and experienced in my family *(Ex.14:24-27)*.

- I speak to the Dawn to take its rightful place, take my family by the edges and shake the wicked out *(Job 38:12-13)*.

- Lord shake all the false foundations of idolatry, false prophets, injustice, occultism, witchcraft and greed out of my bloodline *(Psalm 11:3; 68:1-2)*.

THE LATE MORNING OR FIRST WATCH OF THE DAY

(6.00 AM - 9.00 AM)

Time to Arise and Shine for your Light has Come!

Why would God send us into where we work? Why would he plant us in the neighborhood that we live in? Why would he connect us with the relatives that we have?

IT'S THAT ALL MIGHT BELIEVE!

Isaiah 60:1 in the Amplified Bible renders the Lord's command: Arise [from the depression and prostration in which circumstances have kept you—rise to a new life]! Shine (be radiant with the glory of the Lord), for your light has come, and the glory of the Lord has risen upon you!

Jesus is the light that enlightens every person that comes into the world. It is very important that we all grasp this.

We are not mirrors that reflect God, we are a dwelling place a place in which God dwells. We don't shine good SITTING down we shine STANDING up. The posture of standing is the posture of faith.

Jesus is that which comes from the Father. So, the verse says, "Arise get up and shine why? Your light has come, the Glory has risen upon you. The resurrected one is upon you to demonstrate who He is!

So, here's God's promise to us: If we will get up and shine, this is what will happen; His Glory will be seen upon us. What is the Glory? It's the manifested presence of Jesus.

More and more we are going to see in our own lives that where ever we go people will see Jesus why? Because He says His Glory will be seen upon us.

Say this: " His Glory the manifested presence of Jesus will be seen upon me! This is the promise of the Lord. The non-believer will see the light on us and say, "What's that? Every time they are in our presence they will feel his peace and his love.

This is the time that God strengthens Christians.

Time of Declaration, Decrees, and Proclamation

Decree means to give an official order with the power of legislation issued by a rule or person with authority. We are simply issuing a decree, legislating with an authority given to us by God Himself to bring about His already stated divine will.

The will of God is to make an official order, pronouncement, or legal ruling to effect something. When we speak His word which is already established in the heavens, we enforce it through verbal agreement. Our words become the bridge linking heaven and earth. Literally speaking, You can't bind something in time and then have it bound in eternity. We bring the eternity of Heaven to earth and when Heaven is loosed on the earth things have to change. Heaven is the model we are to follow.

God's Word does not return to Him void and He watches over His Word to perform it *(Isaiah 55:11 Jeremiah 1:12)*. It is His job to bring it to pass and our job to release the Word by declaring, decreeing and proclaiming it into the atmosphere.

Jesus has empowered us for the keeping up of order and government, and to see that his laws be duly served.

Proverbs 8:15 Because of me, kings reign, and rulers make decrees.

Therefore, we are to pray:

- I dedicate myself to You this day in spirit, soul and body.

- As I confess and decree Your Word, Holy Spirit help me to bring pleasure to Your heart.

- I experience spiritual strengthening through the power of Your Word, for Your Word does not return void but accomplishes everything it is sent to do.

- Grant unto me a spirit of wisdom and of revelation in the knowledge of Christ for the glory of Your Kingdom.

- Greater is He that is in me than he that is in the world. Jesus has given me power over all the power of the enemy.

- In my business and workplace I am surrounded with favor as a shield.

- I arise and shine, for my light has come.

- I function in intelligence. The Lord gives me the knowledge of witty inventions and causes me to grow in wisdom, in stature, and in favor with God and man.

- In my business and workplace, I am the head and not the tail. I am above and not beneath. The Lord commands blessings upon my business and workplace, and every project that I put my hands to prospers.

- He establishes my business and workplace as holy unto Himself.

- I decree that Jesus Christ is Lord over my life, business and workplace!

THE EXIT AND ENTRY WATCH OR SECOND WATCH OF THE DAY

(9.00 AM-12.00 Noon)

Time for a harvest of God's promises

The watchman guards and watches for the Word of the Lord to be fulfilled. This is the time to expect the manifestation of God's promises for your life.

Harvest is a time of celebration, marking the end of a growing season and a time of feasting on the fruits of our labors.

"Harvest time." For the most part, throughout the Scriptures, harvest time is associated with gladness and joy. In Jewish history, it was a time of celebration and feast. In the Old Testament, the Feast of Pentecost is called the "Feast of Harvest, the first fruits of your labors which you have sown in the field" (*Exodus 23:16*)

What does it mean to harvest?
Wikipedia, the free encyclopedia says this:
Harvest is the process of gathering mature crops

from the fields. Reaping is the cutting of grain or pulse for harvest, typically using a scythe, sickle, or reaper. The harvest marks the end of the growing season, or the growing cycle for a particular crop.

In our spiritual lives, we might see harvest as the "hard work" of our own spiritual growth and maturity.

So, what's our role in the harvest?
We must understand that Harvest has a process. Just like working in the field we must plow and work the ground if we are going to prepare for a harvest.

Time to be Equipped

Acts 2:15 says it was the *"third hour of the day"* (or 9:00 A.M.) when the Holy Spirit descended in the Upper Room on the day of Pentecost to equip the 120 disciples for service. Pentecost presents us with an opportunity to consider how we are living each day. Are we relying on the power of God's Spirit? Are we an open channel for the Spirit's gifts? Are we attentive to the guidance of the Holy Spirit? Is the fruit of the Spirit (love, joy, peace, etc.) growing in our lives?

As you step out, ask God to equip you for the day, and the descent of the Holy Spirit at Pentecost.

Prayer for Provision to do God's Work
(Exodus 11:3-4)

This is the time to receive the supply of all resources needed for every God-given project *(Exodus 12:35-36).* It was the time that the Israelites got everything that they had to use to build the Tabernacle in the wilderness. Pray for the provision to accomplish whatever God wants you to do.

Time to appropriate the benefits of the Cross (healing, prosperity, forgiveness, strength, etc.). Jesus was crucified at the third hour, or 9:00 A.M. *(Mark 15:25, Matthew 27:45).* After having been on the cross for three hours, darkness came upon the face of the earth at 12:00 P.M. and continued until 3:00 P.M., when the period of darkness ended. Did you notice that even God worked according to the watches of the day, especially pertaining to the crucifixion events?

Prayer for a crucified life.

It is generally accepted that this time period marked both Christ's sentencing by Pilate and His crucifixion. Because of the crucifixion, let us ask God to help us manifest all of the values of a crucified life, by mortifying the deeds of our flesh as stated in *Romans 8:12-15*. This is the time to put off the old man and put on the Lord Jesus Christ *(Colossians 3:2-11).* This is the time to nail witchcraft, bitterness, jealousy, anger, backbiting, gossip, slander, lying, deception, hypocrisy and all the properties and personality traits of the devil and all the works of the flesh to the Cross *(Galatians 2:20; 5:19-21).*

Prayer for Forgiveness, Healing of Relationships and the Release of Others
"Forgive Us for our Trespasses...as We Forgive..." This is the best time to pray this portion of the model prayer the Lord Jesus Christ taught His disciples. In other words it is time to pray for Healing of Relationships. Let this power of love and unity (in one accord) produce the same effect of people asking,

"How come that we all hear them speaking in our own language?"

Therefore, we are to:

- Holy Spirit empowers me to be the Lord's witness even unto the uttermost parts of the earth.

- These signs follow me as I go because I believe.

- The works that Jesus does, I do also in His name and even greater works I do because He has gone to the Father.

- I apply the finished work of the cross to every situation (healing, deliverance, etc.)

- I lift up the voice of the blood on my behalf and in my circumstances so I will operate in the perfect will of the Lord.

- In Jesus' name, I break off any limitations and barriers placed on my life by the works of darkness and evil spirits.

- I bind up and cast off all python and restricting spirits, for God did not give me a spirit of fear, but of power, love, and a sound mind. Romans 8:15; 2 Timothy 1:7

- The Lord shall increase me more and more, me and my children. Psalm 115:14

- I ask to be filled with the Holy Spirit: the Spirit of the Lord, the Spirit of wisdom and understanding, the Spirit of counsel and might, the Spirit of knowledge and fear of the Lord. Ephesians 5:18; Isaiah 11:2

- Now I can do all things through Christ who strengthens me, I can do exceedingly abundantly above all that I ask or think according to the power that works in us, the power of the Holy Spirit. Philippians 4:13; Ephesians 3:20-21

THE WATCH OF SHAKING THE FOUNDATIONS & JUDGMENT

(12:00 Noon - 3:00 PM)

This is the watch that introduces the Midday, otherwise known as the Noon, or the Sixth Hour or the Fullness of Day.

Midday is an hour of rest and a time to seek the Lord. Historically, Christ was on the cross atoning for the sins of the world. Redemption as well as restoration for mankind manifests as a result of what Christ did on the cross.*(Matt.27:45)* Peter received the vision of the clean and unclean animals which initiated the inclusion of the Gentiles in God's redemptive plan.*(Acts 10:9)* Also, it was during this watch that Daniel always went home to pray. *(Note: It is not mentioned at what time in the day Daniel thus kneeled and prayed, but we may presume that it was evening, and morning, and noon. Thus the Psalmist says: "Evening, and morning, and at noon, will I pray, and cry aloud; and he shall hear my voice" Psalm 55:17.)*

This is the time that the promises of God are released and foundations are shaken to exercise your God-given dominion.

Both the midday and the midnight are very important.

The Secret Place

This is very important to pray in line with *Acts 10:9* and *Psalm 91:5, 6, and 14*. It is the time to pray to dwell in the secret place of the Most High, abiding under the shadow of the Almighty, and making the Most High your habitation.

This is the time the Lord truly wants to open up to us, and reveal that which is of the deepest part of His heart. The Lord wants to pour out His wisdom upon us. The Lord will use us mightily, but we must always yield to Him in obedience no matter what the price or what man may say. Be bold and be strong for the Lord is with us, and He will accomplish through us His mission that He has called us to.

As we position ourselves to receive in His Presence, we then can pour out upon others. Staying before the Lord will transform us and usher us into our calls and destinies. *2 Corinthians 3:18 But we all, with unveiled face, beholding as in a mirror the glory of the Lord, are being transformed into the same image from glory to glory, just as by the Spirit of the Lord.*

In seeking Him and beholding Him, we become like Him. By staying in the secret place with God, we find our true identity and destiny. Don't compare yourself to another. The Lord's call is unique and specifically designed for your life. As you stay in His Presence, you will find clarity of mind and blessings that overflow into the lives of others.

To dwell means to sit down and to be sat. Those who make themselves comfortable and stay for a while being willing to take a seat not rushing. Don't just give God five minutes on your way out the door. We need to sit down and make ourselves at home with the Lord. We need to remain and be inhabited and intimate with Him. The secret place is a place of secrecy, a hiding place, a covered shelter where everyone can't go. Only those willing to worship the Father in spirit and in truth for He seeketh such.

Shall abide means to pass the night and remain no matter what.

Almighty- El Shaddai only appeared certain times in the bible. "All Sufficient" You can find sufficiency in God for everything. "Many Breasted" There's room for all of us, anyone willing to dwell in the secret place. The full meaning of El Shaddai is, He is the God of utter ruin and devastation and He is here to do for us what we cannot do for ourselves.

It is also the time of exercising your God given dominion, operating in love and receiving a divine lift, and letting your light shine brighter until the full light of day is attained *(Prov. 4:18)*.

The midday is the fullness of the day and it is the beginning of the Sixth hour. This is the time that the sun is at its fullest, and should yield its optimum best. Pray that the sun will yield its best and precious fruit to you, in line with *Deut. 33:4*. Pray that your life would be bright. This is the time to pray not to be led into any temptation, trap or snare of the enemy.

Pray against Destruction that stalks at noon time. *(Psalm 91:5)* Destruction is released at midday according to *Psalm 92:6-7*. Pray and cut off all satanic arrows that are released at this time. This is the time Justice shall come to you *(Isa. 7:14).* Pray that the mystery of the secret place of the Most High would begin to speak.

Pray that the sun will yield its best and precious fruit to you, in line with Deut. 33:14. *"And for the precious fruits brought forth by the sun, and for the precious things put forth by the moon"* Pray that your life would be bright.

This is the time to pray not to be led into any temptation, trap or snare of the enemy.

The destruction that stalks at noon time.

Pray and cut off all satanic arrows that are released at this time. This is the time Justice shall come to you *(Isa. 7:14).*

Destruction is released at midday according to *Psalm 92:6-7.* The meaning is, that whenever, or in whatever form, calamity comes whether at midnight or at noon - whether in the form of pestilence, war, or famine - he who trusts in God need not be afraid. He will feel either that he will be preserved from its ravages, or that if he is cut off he has nothing to fear. The Latin Vulgate says this, "Nor of mischance and the demon of noonday."

We must not listen to the voice of the enemy or fall into the deceits
and the deceptions of his lies but we must walk in truth. There is great peace and security in truth. The Lord will save us from the entanglements, and snares and traps of the enemy. The truth will set us free from the fear of failure. When led by the Lord we will be victorious. If God be for us who can rise up against us?

So, stand up and shine! Rise to a new life! Be radiant with the Glory of His presence! For the Glory is upon you!

Therefore, we are to pray:
- Father, in the Name of Jesus, I thank You that You watch over Your Word to perform it.

- I praise You that I dwell in the secret place of the Most High and that I shall remain stable and fixed under the shadow of El Shaddai.

- I will say of You, Lord, "The Lord is my refuge and my fortress, my God; on Him I lean and rely, and in Him I confidently trust!"

- For then You will deliver me from the snare of the fowler and from the deadly pestilence.

- Then You will cover me with Your feathers, and under Your wings shall I trust and find refuge. May the protection of the Lord become the portion of your household.

- Your truth and Your faithfulness are a shield and a buckler.

- You are my confidence, firm and strong. You keep my foot from stumbling, being caught in a trap

- You give me safety and ease me. I know You will keep me in perfect peace because my mind is stayed on You and I trust in You.

- Lord protect and gladden my heart. Overthrow the stronghold of my enemies and may they be overthrown without pity *(Jer. 20:16).*

- My healing comes quickly like the dawn. My path shines even brighter till the full of day *(Prov. 4:18)*.

- When I lie down You will give me peaceful sleep, for You sustain me and make me dwell in safety.

- I shall not be afraid of the terror of the night, nor of the arrow (the evil plots and slanders of the wicked) that flies by day, nor of the pestilence that stalks in darkness, nor of the destruction and sudden death that surprise and lay waste at noonday.

- A thousand may fall at my side, and ten thousand at my right hand, but it shall not come near me. Only a spectator shall I be—inaccessible in the secret place of the Most High—as I witness the reward of the wicked.

THE TRANSFORMATION WATCH OR FOURTH WATCH

(3:00 PM - 6:00 PM)

This watch ushers in and begins at the hour of prayer according to *Acts 3:1, Acts 10:30, Isa. 60:11-22.* The one single most important characteristic or practice that identifies the church is Prayer. The most important privilege of the entire church is prayer and the only hour in the Bible that is specifically referred to as the Hour of Prayer begins at 3:00 PM. This was the time that the veil in front of the Holy of Holies tore from top to bottom. This watch is therefore the time for access!

Hour of Prayer

This time is an hour of Revelation, hour of Grace, hour of Removing Veils *(Luke 23:45-46),* hour of Power, hour of Glory, hour of the voice of the Lord, hour of Triumph. This is the time to die to the world (self). This time is also the time of seeking the Lord in Truth. This is the hour of the establishment of the Kingdom, why? Righteousness and Justice are the foundation of His Throne. This is the time when Jesus said "It is finished." At 3:00 pm Jesus gave up the ghost. Jesus went through

6 hours of suffering for the deliverance of humankind and the universe. Pray for **deliverance** during this watch. It is also the time for the miraculous and angelic visitation *(Zech. 1:10-11, 18-21).* This time also the time of the evening sacrifice. It was at this time that Elijah called forth fire from Heaven to consume the prophets of Baal on Mt. Carmel *(1 Kings 18:29, 30, 36-39).*

Covenant

Throughout the history of God's dealings with man, He has revealed Himself as a covenant-making God. The Almighty covenanted with Noah, Abraham, Moses and David; He renewed His Abrahamic covenant in His call to Isaac and Jacob. Each covenant initiated a new wave of redemptive power into the world and forever impacted the human condition.

The word *covenant* means "to fetter" or chain together. It was the highest form of commitment that two individuals could share.

When the Lord initiated His covenant with a man, He did so as an extension of His eternal purpose. Contained within the Lord's covenant was His divine intervention, His supernatural wisdom and strategies, and His provisions.

Our salvation has been secured, not only because Jesus died for our sins, but because His death was part of a covenant He had with the Father.

A covenant with God accomplishes two interconnected goals. It thrusts us beyond "subjective prayer" (prayer made primarily for our personal needs), and it brings us into a deeper commitment to God. Out of greater commitment comes greater grace to accomplish God's redemptive work in the world. An example of covenant power is seen in ancient Israel during the revival that occurred after Athaliah, an idolatrous Judean queen, was dethroned. Jehoiada, the high priest, looked to God in covenant prayer. We read, *"Then Jehoiada made a covenant between the Lord and the king and the people, that they should be the Lord's people" (2 Kings 11:17).*

The result of his covenant was that grace came upon the people and they cleansed the land of idolatry. We read, "So all the people of the land rejoiced and the city was quiet" (v. 20). Jehoiada's covenant brought the nation back to God and ended violence in Jerusalem!

Consider also the power released in Hezekiah's covenant with God. The nation of Judah had been fully corrupted by Ahaz, the preceding king. However, Hezekiah began his reign by seeking God's highest favor. He opened the doors of the temple and re-consecrated the priests.

Yet, the purification of priests and buildings by themselves would not have brought about revival had not Hezekiah taken one further step. He said, *"Now it is in my heart to make a covenant with the Lord God of Israel, that His burning anger may turn away from us" (2 Chr. 29:10).*

Just eight days after the king made a covenant with the Lord, we read, *"Then Hezekiah and all the people rejoiced over what God had prepared for the people, because the thing came about suddenly"* (v. 36). The difference between a long-term struggle and a speedy turning of the nation was, I believe, in the power that was released when the king covenanted with the Almighty.

Power of Love

God's love is limitless-hotter than fire and stronger than anything. Look at the power in these words: *"I am convinced that nothing will ever separate us from God's love. Neither death nor life, neither angels or demons, neither our fears for today nor our worries about tomorrow-not even the powers of Hell can separate us from the God's love. No power in the sky above or in the earth below-indeed, nothing in all creation will ever be able to separate us from the love of God that is revealed in Christ Jesus our Lord" (Romans 8:38-39 NLT).*

How deep is the Father's love for us? His unfailing love is as high as the heavens and reaches to the sky (see *Psalm 57:10*). His love is unconditional, meaning it has no conditions. God does not put stipulations on His love. His love is real, limitless, and changeless. It is the only love we do not have to earn in some way.

When Christ told us to bless those who curse us, it was for our sake, it was to protect our hearts from cold love.

The stronger our ability to forgive and even bless those who've been a curse to us, the stronger our love will be-the greater the impact God will have through us.

When you want to hate but love instead through God's power, you unlock the richness of Heaven. You unleash God's power on yourself and those around you!

Triumphant Glory

The anointing is here, today, for us to overcome and be triumphant! An anointing is here now for victory!

God wants to give authority to His people-- authority which is our God-given right--that, when exercised, will overcome the devil and all the warfare that is against us. This is a God-given right for believers, and corporately for the church, so that both come to a new place in the spirit, far above powers, principalities, and the warfare sent against us.

God is going to bring the breakthrough all the way through--*"Through God we will do valiantly, for it is He who shall tread down our enemies" (Psalms 60:12).* Let's declare the words of David from *Psalms: 68:1: "Let God arise, let His enemies be scattered; let those also who hate Him flee before Him."* But let's not forget that simultaneously, as God brings the breakthrough, He wants to train our hands for war and our fingers for battle *(Psalms 144:1). "He teaches my hands to make war, so that my arms can bend a bow of bronze" (Psalms 18:34).* As we allow God to train us in warfare we'll be wearing those "robes of authority for those who overcome."

It's vital that we learn how to overcome. God wants us to see that we are more than conquerors through Him *(Romans 8:37).*

Time to Change/ Shape History

This was the time God changed history because this watch happens to be the time that Jesus gave up the ghost with a loud voice. When Jesus gave up the ghost, history was changed forever because He now cut a covenant for us with God and there was a triumphant Glory over hell, death and the grave and the Bible says at that hour darkness departed.

We, Christians, are "the Church", and the church is meant to be a manifestation of Jesus, doing what He did, the way that He did it: healing the sick, casting out devils, performing signs and wonders. We see that the apostle Paul, in his letter to the Ephesians, was challenging the believers like this: "Guys, you are never going to start operating in resurrection power and start operating in the miracles of Jesus until you have a revelation of the exceeding greatness of His power towards us who believe." I want you to think about that!

Such revelation will absolutely transform you, and you'll experience "what you are becoming" as you go and do the stuff. So hang on! We're on the verge of seeing the victorious, triumphant church in operation! Really, the best is yet to come!

Therefore, we are to pray:

- Ask the Lord to remove every obstacle and hindrance from your heart and mind so you will be free to seek Him, and call upon him as a good son relates to his Father.
- Pray that God will redeem our spiritual sight from all the things that have blindfolded us from seeing visions of God *(Acts 10:3-10, Isa. 44:17-18).*
- Ask God to clear your heart and mind of filth and spiritual garbage so you will be at liberty to receive divine dreams, revelations and insight from the Spirit of God *(Acts 10:10-11).*
- Pray for open heavens so you will be ushered into the presence of God as a laborer for the kingdom *(Daniel 6:13).*
- Pray for an encounter with God.
- Distraction is the enemy of our soul. Pray that God will deal with all demonic transactions in our hearts,

minds, emotions, wills and bodies; that distract us from focusing on God's purposes *(Matt. 21:12)*.

- Pray that the Lord will find you ready when he comes for the church. Ask Him to grant you the wisdom to put oil in your lamp, and even hold some in reserve, so you will have the stamina to wait for Him *(Luke 12:38, 35)*.

In Conclusion:

We become a prophetic voice when we proclaim and declare God's will, and pray it out in the atmosphere.

It's time to use prayer to turn the tables on the enemy. We can make the devil tired, weary, depressed, discouraged, exhausted, and in need of psychiatric care. In fact, we can wear him out exactly as he has worn out the Church.

I love the example Jesus gives us in Luke 22:31-32

"Simon, Simon, Satan has asked to have all of you, to sift you like wheat. But I have pleaded in prayer for you, Simon, that your faith should not fail. So when you have repented and turned to me again, strengthen and build up your brothers."

Jesus could have simply taken authority over the enemy and prevented the situation from actually happening. However, He recognized that it was important for Simon Peter to struggle through to a deeper place of faith and relationship. Simon had to discover something profound about himself and also the love of

God for him. God wants us to know what He is praying.

What's the conversation in Heaven over your life right now? Unlocking the gates of the watch allows us to rise above our circumstances and pray in line with a God who adores us, and wants us to be supremely confident in doing His will. He wants us to find joy in our situation and to understand that there's nothing out there that can harm us, because of who He is in us.

Let's be confident and focus on God so that the enemy cannot trap us in fear and doubt.

About the Author

Malinda V. Robinson was born in Newport News, VA at the historic black hospital, Whitaker Memorial Hospital in 1966. Her family lived in the Ridley Circle community and later moved to the Newsome Park area. In 1971 the family moved to Hampton, VA where Malinda graduated from Hampton High School in 1985.

Throughout her life he has been continually placed in leadership positions: scholastic honors classes in during grade school, school safety patrol, ROTC Officer, Student Council in grade school, Candy Stripper in a youth volunteer program which landed her first job working at Newport News General Hospital as a Registration Clerk.

Her interests are broad and varied. For example, she traveled to Jamaica where she taught youth bible study for three weeks during the summer. While in Jamaica, she volunteered in a restoration project that would assist in aiding children at death and blind school. She participated for two summers and it was there that she heard the Lord speak to her regarding His plan for her life.

She earned her M.Ed. in 2000 from Carolina University of Theology, her B. A., in 1997 from Carolina University of Theology. She studied business administration at Norfolk State University in 1988 and went on to complete course work at Thomas Nelson Community College.

In April of 1997 she married her soul mate and best friend Kenneth L. Robinson. They have two beautiful children KJ and Kenya. The family resides in Hampton, VA.

Malinda has worked extensively in matters involving negotiations in staffing, human resources and training. She has also taught in the private elementary and secondary education arena as well as the collegiate levels of education.

Malinda has written and lectured on various training materials relating to human resource topics. While working at Northrop Grumman, Newport News she developed a training module designed to help welding graduates transition into the day to day operations within the steal and fabrications division.

Malinda currently leads the workforce ministry at Empowered Believers Christian Learning Center where we encourage, train, and support believers in the work place.

When she is not working, she loves to read, to travel and to learn.

You may contact her at the following:

- Kingdom In You Ministry Network, 22 W Big Sky Drive, Hampton, VA 23666, 757-513-8859
- Empowered Believers Christian Learning Center, 2096 Nickerson Blvd, Hampton, VA 23669, 757-240-5834

www.ingramcontent.com/pod-product-compliance
Lightning Source LLC
Chambersburg PA
CBHW071145090426

42736CB00012B/2229